TEXTBOOK
AMY
KROUSE
ROSENTHAL

DUTTON
⟶ est. 1852 ⟵

An imprint of Penguin Random House LLC
375 Hudson Street
New York, New York 10014

Permissions can be found on page iv.

LIBRARY OF CONGRESS CATALOGING-IN-PUBLICATION DATA
has been applied for.

ISBN 978-1-101-98454-3

Printed in the United States of America
1   3   5   7   9   10   8   6   4   2
Set in Minion Pro and Playfair Display

TEXTBOOK AMY KROUSE ROSENTHAL

AMY KROUSE ROSENTHAL

DUTTON
— est. 1852 —

CONDITION OF BOOK

__ New
__ Signed edition
__ Used, like new
__ Used, like used

ANY ADDITIONAL NOTES: _____

_____

CONDITION OF AUTHOR

__ Pretty bad
_X_ Pretty good

ANY ADDITIONAL NOTES: At present, the author is in relatively good condition. She exercises regularly—a combination of long walks, swimming, and weight training to retain bone density— and enjoys a well-balanced diet, though it is noted she could cut back on cheese. She is able to run upstairs to grab something real quick without getting too out of breath. In a pinch, she could fill in as your tennis doubles partner. Her hearing: fine. Her eyesight: eh. One last final inspection revealed a couple minor scratches on her lower left leg, and a three-millimeter rip on her right earlobe, presumably due to large, heavy earrings worn in her youth.

THE HUMAN CONDITION

_X_ Gosh, that's a tough one.

ANY ADDITIONAL NOTES: Existence is akin to a 300,000-hours-long game of whack-a-mole where the grand prize dangling in the back row is your inevitable death. But I'll tell you what: On any given day, you sure can find a nice array of free, tasty samples at the grocery store.

ISSUED TO: _____   **DATE:** _____

SUGGESTED READING

This book.

Contents

I would like to acknowledge that the following have earned extra credit:

agent Amy Rennert	for absolutely everything.
collaborators Ruby Western and Kayla Ginsburg	for everything that led to here.
colleagues Emily Snyder, Nick Gage, Brian Stojak, and Baize Buzan	for everything before that.
corn bread	for how amazing you smell baking in the oven. Sometimes I don't fully notice until I step outside to grab the mail and walk back in.
friend David	for saying the following after I texted you a photo of me standing in front of our old hangout: *Hey—could you do me a favor while you are there? I accidentally left something right around that spot a while back... my youth. If you could look around for it, that'd be a big help. It was last seen in baggy jeans, smoking a cigarette, and making big plans.*
man at the corner of Ashland and Addison	for what you did on Saturday, February 15, 2014, at 7:45pm. Jason and I were walking to meet some friends for dinner. It was a cold and snowy night. Foolishly hatless, I was walking down the street covering my ears with my mittened hands. While waiting for the light to change, you approached us and asked, *Ma'am, would you like this hat?* as you pulled off and offered your own.

cont'd.

Krouses Ann, Paul, Beth, Joe, and Katie	for *glorious, glorious.*
offspring Justin, Miles, and Paris	for R's.
mate Jason	for ever.
receptionist at doctor's office	for saying, sure, I could listen in. (When I was checking in for my appointment, you were starting to tell the other receptionist about a crazy dream you had the night before.) You dreamt you were dying. Your boss was throwing you, literally and morbidly, a going-away party. Your coworkers made you a cake. Suddenly you realized that your mom was a no-show. You couldn't believe she bailed on your farewell lunch. Then your boyfriend said to you, *Well, the coroner's here. You better jump in the bag now.* You woke up, crying. You immediately called your mom to confirm that if she knew you were dying, she would totally meet you for lunch.
taxi driver who took us to the airport	for being so cool and understanding when we finally tracked you down on the phone and told you it wasn't until we were checking in at the ticket counter that we realized we had mistakenly grabbed your briefcase, thinking it was Jason's. You and I decided the only solution at this point was for your briefcase to accompany us on vacation.

cont'd.

tech company OneReach	for bringing the texting component to interactive life.
web developer Zac Davis	for building the book's online home.
Jill, Ruby, Kayla, and Merrill	for being word-Smiths.
team Dutton	for believing in, bettering, and publishing this book.
philosopher Wittgenstein	for saying this: *The aspects of things that are most important for us are hidden because of their simplicity and familiarity. One is unable to notice something because it is always before one's eyes.*

INTRODUCTION

Welcome to the first book that offers additional engagement via texting.

You will find texting interactions sprinkled throughout this book. You can choose to participate in all, some, or none.

Rest assured this book functions perfectly fine without the texting element, just like any other "normal" book.

If you do partake in these interactive interludes, you may choose to do so in real time as you read, or you may choose to come back to any of them later—whatever you wish.

To begin, simply text **Hello** to **312-883-9945**.

You will receive a greeting from me, Amy, confirming you are good to go.

P.S. Will you receive any random, unsolicited, out-of-the-blue texts? No way. That's pretty much the exact opposite of what this experience is all about.

FIG.1

In case you're reading this book in Antartica/in space/in the distant future, please know that the texting component is limited by geography, volume, and the passage of time. You can always swing by textbookamykr.com to see how these texting interactions with readers are playing out.

INTRODUCTION

Why the title *Textbook Amy Krouse Rosenthal*?

Because a *textbook* is a literary work about a
particular subject.

Because *textbook* would accurately describe a book with an
interactive text-messaging component.

Because *textbook* is an expression meaning "quintessential,"
"definitive," "classic example"—*Oh, that wordplay and whole
unconventional format is so typical of her, so textbook Amy K.R. . . .
give me a break.*

Because if an author's previous book has
Encyclopedia in the title (*Encyclopedia of an Ordinary Life*),
following it up ten years later with a
Textbook would be rather nice.

The Central Characters in This Book

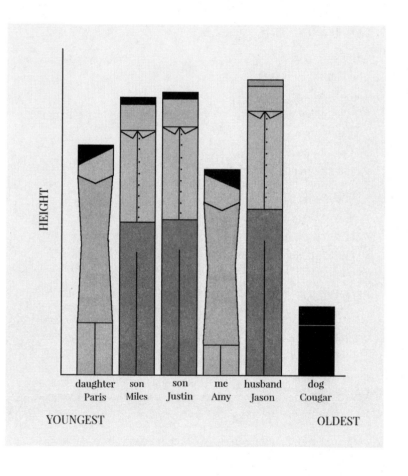

PRE-ASSESSMENT

I AM READING THIS

- in bed.
- in transit.
- on the beach.
- in a bookstore, head slightly cocked to the side, trying to decide what to make of it.

I AM READING THIS BOOK BECAUSE

- my book group chose it.
- my professor assigned it.
- it was recommended by a friend whose opinion I value.
- it has appeared.

PEOPLE SAY

- I am very, very funny.
- I am medium funny.
- I am not that funny.

MY GENERAL STATE OF MIND AS IT PERTAINS TO WANTING IS

- I have enough, I'm good.
- I have enough, but I'd like just a wee bit more.
- I do not have enough.
- Actually, I have more than enough and could probably do with less.

IN GROUP DISCUSSIONS

- I truly want to hear what others have to say and enjoy listening.
- I theoretically want to hear what others have to say, yet I find myself doing most of the talking.
- I want others to hear what I have to say, but I seem to have difficulty inserting/asserting myself.
- I want others to hear what I have to say and have no problem whatsoever making that happen.

I'M TRYING

- to understand.
- to remember.
- to forget.
- my best.

I TEND TO

- have trouble with ceiling fan strings. Pull it once to stop? Twice? In trying to turn it off, I will just speed it up—great, now it is spinning around so fast that it's wobbling almost violently.
- buy a headband every couple years thinking it might finally look good on me. It never looks good. It should be clear by now that as much as I would like it to be so, I am not a headband person.
- marvel at the sight of a portable wooden box displaying an orderly panoply of teas.
- feel at this stage of my life that we are all the same age: 20 years younger? 20 years older? We are the same. 9 years old? Me too! 95? Me too!

I LIKE YOU BECAUSE

- you are nice.
- you have a way about you.
- I feel good when I'm around you.
- you get it.

I MAY ALSO LIKE YOU SIMPLY BECAUSE

- you waved thank you in the rearview mirror when I let you in the lane.
- you like me.

NO OFFENSE BUT I DO NOT LIKE

- overly chatty salespeople.
- salespeople who use an unnaturally high, fake-nice voice.
- when salespeople say, *Thank you for your patience.*
  I want to say, *I was not at all patient; I had no choice here.*

EVERYONE BUT ME REALLY SEEMS TO BE INTO

- spaghetti and meatballs.
- going to the midnight showing of *The Rocky Horror Picture Show* in college. I always fell asleep.
- asking and answering the question *So, how was your weekend?* Thankfully by two o'clock or so on Monday afternoon it always dies down.
- knickknacks.

IF

- a = b and b = c, then a = c.
- you're happy and you know it, clap your hands.

PLEASE DO NOT ASK ME TO

○ hold my applause until the very end. It feels unnatural, rude even. I really want to clap for each award winner or graduate. I can practically feel the suppressed desire in my palms, like the push/pull tension of two positive magnets. Furthermore, it just must be such an anticlimactic bummer, exiting the stage like that, in awkward, applause-less silence.

○ have sex in the lavatory.

○ set an intention for my yoga practice.

CHAIRS ARE GREAT BECAUSE

○ you can stand on them to reach things.

○ if you have company you can just bring extra ones out from the closet.

○ there are so many different, pretty kinds.

○ you can lean back on two legs and just catch yourself.

○ some swivel, and that's fun.

○ you can come home and throw your jacket on the back.

○ they are quiet.

FIG.1 FIG.2 FIG.3 FIG.4 FIG.5 FIG.6 FIG.7

MY MAIL CARRIER'S NAME IS

- Mary.
- not Mary.

MY KEYS

- are right where I left them.
- must be in my other coat.
- . . . Your guess is as good as mine.

HAROLD

- and the Purple Crayon.
- and Maude.

FOR SOME REASON, IT TAKES MY BRAIN A MOMENT TO PROCESS

- that red means hot and blue means cold.
- the open-close symbols on elevators, which is which.
- that the delivery truck in front of me said *party linens*, not *panty liners*.

I WOULD REALLY RATHER NOT

- reciprocate out of obligation.
- sponge the outside of the Cuisinart.
- fall from grace.

I CANNOT BE THE ONLY ONE WHO

- thinks that Christo must wrap gifts incredibly well.
- finds it slightly self-important to sign emails with one's initials.
- suspects the opera box is precariously attached and might snap off at any moment.
- hopes if I ever had to share a jail cell, it would be with someone who likes to give back rubs.
- is convinced I can still make it work when clearly the Velcro buckle has lost its fastening oomph.
- feels that both rain and pomegranate balsamic are nice as a light drizzle.
- finds myself making a concerted effort to heave/tug/lug a conversation up and over the hill of small talk.
- when pressing the spoon along the perforated lines of the Pillsbury Cinnamon Rolls tube and anticipating what's about to happen is still—yikes!—startled when it pops open, despite having done this a million times.
- draws a little arrow directing the recipient to the back of the greeting card, as if the recipient couldn't figure out what to do next without my direction, as if the recipient would give up, figuring I had just abandoned the card midsentence.
- feels it is important to say good-bye to hotel rooms before vacating.
- enjoys when my hand slips into the pocket of a coat I haven't worn in a while and I am unexpectedly reunited with a small but pleasing item, like a favorite hair scrunchie, lip balm, or that one good pen.

WHEN I'M THOROUGHLY ENJOYING MYSELF AT A LARGE ARENA SPORTING EVENT OR CONCERT,

- I leave early. Why would I want to risk dealing with the parking lot traffic?
- I stay to the very end. Why would I want to miss a single minute?

LOOKING AT THE FOLLOWING SYMBOLS, THE FIRST WORDS THAT SPRING TO MIND ARE

- peace, love, yay, swirly, la la la, bloom, sun.
- war, broken, danger, dizzy, off-key, wilt, fading star.

YOU CAN ALWAYS COUNT ON ME TO

- be a responsible, empathic citizen of the world.
- pick up a stray thread on the floor.
- fall asleep during savasana.
- return your Tupperware.

IT IS

- one thing to accumulate woes bit by bit over the course of a lifetime.
- quite another to enter this world with impossible burdens, by no doing of your own, and find yourself unequipped to handle them and/or find that, despite every conceivable effort, they are mercilessly unshakable.

I HAVE BEEN WAITING

- for you at the northeast corner, by the Starbucks, as we agreed.
- for you to notice that I do not care.
- for someone like you.

YOU

- make me not afraid of getting old.

LATELY I FEEL

- full of longing.
- fragile and uncertain.
- centered, electric, brave, and alive.

FINALLY, IT IS MY UNDERSTANDING THAT AMY

- wants to give me something useful and beautiful.
- suspects she may never be able to do this again.
- sends me off with her love. ∎

GEOGRAPHY

My father-in-law tells me his Pal story. He was a young boy out on a field trip with his class. He suddenly saw his dog Pal and their dog walker across the way. *Hey, that's my dog, everyone! That's my dog Pal!* he shouted to his teacher and classmates. He wanted, of course, to run over, but his teacher insisted he remain in line. All these years later, the thing he remembers most is how incredibly weird it was to see Pal when he was out on this field trip.

He says he hadn't thought about the Pal story in years but was reminded of it a few days ago when something similar happened. He was cruising along Lake Shore Drive when (again, out of the blue) he spotted his youngest son, Tony, driving in the opposite direction. *Oh my gosh, there's my son! There he goes!* he thought to himself as they whizzed by each other. He said it was a quintessential Pal moment—being out and about in the universe, and then unexpectedly crossing paths with someone from home base.

It seems this sensation can also apply to home base itself. I am now remembering being on a walking architectural tour of Chicago in my early twenties and being surprised when the guide not only ushered the group down my street but then also stopped in front of the very four-flat where I lived. The building survived the Great Chicago Fire and had landmark status. I kept motioning to the other people in my group, *That's my house! This is where I live!* I had deliberately wandered away from home for the afternoon, and to have it presented to me in this manner was exhilarating. ■

I was at a water park with the kids. I found myself at the top of the park's highest and steepest slide. I was scared. I kept motioning people to go ahead of me. *Okay, he didn't die. Okay, she didn't die either.* The succession of non-deaths was comforting but not convincing. The kids were all wading/waiting for me at the bottom. *Come on, Mom!* I forced myself to lie down in the arms-crossed-over-chest position. *Ready?* asked the lifeguard. I shut my eyes tight. *Yeah, I'm ready.* Right away I felt an enormous sense of relief. *This isn't bad at all*, I thought. *It's a shockingly smooth ride.* I thought about what great engineering was behind this contraption. I was flying down so fast it hardly felt like I was moving. I was stunned when I heard the lifeguard's voice again. *Ma'am, would you like a push?* ∎

I had a dream I was on *Fresh Air.* After her signature introduction—*from WHYY in Philadelphia, I'm Terry Gross with* (PAUSE AND ENTHUSIASTIC LILT) Fresh Air*!*— she turned to me and asked, *So, what are your thoughts about the election?* I sighed and said, *Can't we talk about something beautiful, Terry? Like the nice sound you can make by circling your finger around the rim of a wineglass?* ◼

To hear a few renditions of a humming wineglass, text **Cheers**.

One is performed by a Master Sommelier,

one by me, and one by my cousin,

whose name is also Terry Gross.

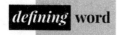

serendipity

1. If you like something, you tend to be on the lookout for it. And if you're on the lookout for it, you tend to find it, or it—*Yoo-hoo! Over here!*—finds you. And so it goes, for me, with serendipity and coincidence. It's something I like, so it's something I notice and attract.

2. People often share anecdotes with me. *I know you will appreciate this*, they say. Indeed, I can be counted on to validate the remarkableness of their tales, bringing my hands to my cheeks

24

and exclaiming in all the right places. I feign nothing. Even people I am meeting for the first time (but who are familiar with my work and leanings—it's not exactly a subtle theme) will go straight from a handshake into full-on serendipity story mode. Like Christopher, a bookseller I met on one of my very first book tours. He told me that he was born in Colorado, reminded me that Denver is known as the Mile High City, and that a mile is exactly 5,280 feet. Then he revealed his full name and birthday: Christopher Denver from Colorado was born on 5/2/80. It is the one and only thing I remember about that trip.

3. What if, instead of being enchanted by coincidence and serendipity, I was, say, all about rug hooking. I imagine there would be a similar course of events: I'd always be looking for cool rug-hooking kits; I'd eventually amass a decent collection; I'd write an article for a crafting magazine with the title "Rug Hooking . . . Hooked!"; I'd create posts with the hashtag #hugarughooker; people would be excited to show me their rug hook pillows.

4. Years ago I read an article in *The New York Times Sunday Magazine* about the mathematics of coincidence. It was fascinating, and I was happy to find it again online, as fascinating as ever. Lisa Belkin wrote:

Something like that has to be more than coincidence, we protest. What are the odds? The mathematician will answer that even in the most unbelievable situations, the odds are actually very good. . . .

"The really unusual day would be one where nothing unusual happens," explains Persi Diaconis, a Stanford statistician who has spent his career collecting and studying examples of coincidence. Given that there are 280 million people in the United States, he says, "280 times a day, a one-in-a-million shot is going to occur."

5. But still.

6. I want to share this: Jason and I were at an art lecture. The speaker mentioned something

about "Dürer's Rhinoceros," which I had never heard of. Summary: Albrecht Dürer / 16th-century German artist / had never seen a rhinoceros before / drew one based solely on the descriptions of others / keep in mind this was pre-photography. I made a note to read more about this German artist and his famous rhino rendering later. I came home from the event to find a letter waiting for me in the mail. It was from Germany. It was from a group that calls itself the Rhino Pupils.

7. And this: At a book reading, I decided I was going to give away my snowglobe ring to someone in the audience. It wasn't because I didn't love the ring—I actually really, really loved the ring—but rather because I was trying

my hand at nonattachment. I asked, *Who would like this ring?* A couple dozen arms shot up. I then asked those individuals to consider how badly they wanted the ring; if they felt that someone else should maybe have it, would they please put their arm down. A few eager limbs remained in the air. I looked at each person carefully. One woman standing in the back struck me as most needing/wanting the ring. *It's yours*, I said, pointing her way. But I had one request; I asked if she would please pass the ring on to someone else a few months down the road. She agreed. I told her it would be extra great if she could do so on my birthday, April 29th. *No problem*, she said, smiling. *April 29th is my birthday too.*

8. And this: I heard an unusual thump at our front door. If it was a Sunday morning, I might have thought it was a tossed newspaper. But it was a Monday afternoon. When I opened the door and looked down, I realized what had happened: A poor bird had flown into our window. This had never happened before. I quickly found the number for a bird rescue service. They said to bring the bird inside the house and place it gently inside a shoe box. While waiting for them to arrive, I noticed a letter sitting atop a pile of papers on the dining room table. I didn't recognize it, wasn't sure

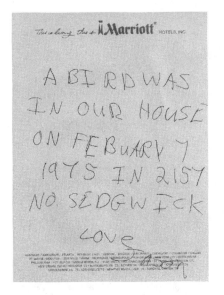

where it had come from, and then I remembered: Over the weekend Jason had been going through a box of childhood mementos. The letter was one he had written nearly forty years ago. In his little-boy handwriting, the note began: *A bird was in our house . . .*

9. And last one for now, this: When Miles was born, my aunt gave me a silver link bracelet engraved with his name and birth date. I put it on and never took it off. Two decades passed. One summer afternoon I was standing in the kitchen, unpacking groceries. Miles was heading back to college soon, returning for his sophomore year. His specific departure and

general growing-up were both weighing heavy on my mind. Like a hand appearing from out of nowhere and resting on my shoulder, my subconscious whispered: *It's time to let him go.* The heartbreaking and nearly audible message stopped me in my tracks. A split second later I heard a clink. I looked down and saw my bracelet in a tiny heap on the counter. All these years, it had never once slipped off, so I was confused. I realized it did not slip off—the clasp had simply worn all the way down. This just happened to be the moment it let go.

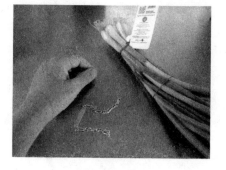

10. About these coincidences, the data and mathematicians are clear: Such things happen all

the time. Then again, Einstein (pretty good at math) was also quite clear when he concluded, *There are only two ways to live your life. One is as though nothing is a miracle. The other is as though everything is a miracle.*

11. I'm going with B, everything. ■

To share a serendipity story from your own life, (and/or view stories from other readers), go to **Serendipity** at textbookamykr.com.

Wyoming is the farthest-away state, Miles told us one night at dinner. He was little, maybe six at the time. We weren't sure what he meant. *Farthest away from where, sweetie?* After some prodding we came to understand his comment and logic: He assumed that Wyoming's position on the map correlated to its alphabetical position (which is to say 50th) among the states. Wyoming was somewhere way out there, the last in line. ■

FIG.1 United States of America in alphabetical order

Jason was biking to work when his contact lens popped out. Within a few seconds, five or six people hopped off their bikes to help him look. The image of this spontaneous, collegial huddle of strangers is worth pausing to fully conjure.

Things were not looking too hopeful. Then: *Got it! Got it!* said one fellow, hand high in the air, lens pinched between fingers. When Jason thanked him, he said, *Hey, no problem. One time I found my friend's contact lens at the bottom of a swimming pool.* Apparently this was the single best person you could possibly hope to run into in such a situation. ■

FIG.1

FIG.2

FIG.3

FIG.4

FIG.5

When I came back from India, I was absolutely, positively 100% sure I was going to use a lot of turmeric. ∎

Short Answer

Our babysitter Emily was at the gas station when she encountered a desperate soul trying to sell a puppy for a few quick bucks; she promptly bought/ rescued the dog. She told me this when she walked in the door that day, adding that the puppy was now safely in her car (windows cracked open) and that she was going to take him to the animal shelter after work. *Would it be okay to bring him in the house?* she asked. Alas, while sleeping dogs lie, I cannot. I did not say, *Of course, Emily, no problem.* What I said was, *I'm sorry, Emily, but I do not want the kids knowing ANYTHING about this dog.* They were 7, 9, and 11 at the time and had been beggggging for a dog for approximately 7, 9, and 11 years. My short answer was always a shade of *no, never*:

> *No, never—you know I don't like dogs.*
> *No, never—I will not be responsible for another living thing.*
> *No, never—I don't even want a plant.*

A couple hours later, the kids were all home from school. Justin had a dog-walking job, so he set off on his usual route around the block. I went into my backyard studio to do some writing. If I were an accountant instead of a writer, perhaps I'd have done a better job of putting two and two together. No sooner had Justin left than he came running back through the door, screaming, *Emily! Emily! There's a puppy in your car! Do you know there's a puppy in your car?! Miles, Paris—Emily has a puppy in her car!*

You can imagine the fanfare and quaint pleading. I fake-listened intently, and then, in the most emphatic way possible, inserted a *nonnegotiable* before my *no, never.*

Jason not only agreed, but if this were a contest, he might have even been crowned hatingest hater.

The next day, I left for an out-of-town work trip. When I called to check in with the kids, I learned—in between their giddy shrieks and me saying *Wait, what? Slow down, slow down!*—that Jason had fallen both a) under a spell and b) in love with the dog. This was very, very not good.

I returned home a few days later. It turned out to be not only the first but also the last time I was unhappy to see Cougar Rosenthal run to the front door to greet me. ■

FIG.1 Amy ♥ Cougar

It takes a snowflake two hours to fall from cloud to earth. Can't you just see its slow, peaceful descent? ∎

Jason and I were in a cab. We came to an intersection with signs on every corner. The sign straight ahead said *DEAD END* (going straight: not an option). The sign to the left said *WRONG WAY* (going left: not an option). The sign to the right said *ONE WAY* (going right: only viable option). The cabdriver was about to go straight. Jason quickly directed him to go left. I believe the exact words I blurted out in exasperated disbelief were: *Guys. Seriously?* ■

Hmmm. That woman stepping out of the shower sure is hairy—my last thought before realizing I had walked into the men's locker room. ■

I read *A Moveable Feast*, Ernest Hemingway's memoir of his writerly life in 1920s Paris, when I was twenty and living in that same city. Every time he wrote about something I recognized or frequented (a street, a monument, a café), I'd enthusiastically underline, highlight, circle, double star. Perhaps taking a cue from Hemingway's first name, I filled the narrow margins with my wide-eyed scrawl. In the end, the book became an annotated, tiered treasure—a travelogue atop a travelogue.

Why I loaned the book to my housemate that spring, I will never know. What I do know is this: It was left on a train, Hadley-style.*

Surely someone came across it that day. Maybe it was handed over to an employee at the station who then sold it for a few francs to a used bookstore. Maybe it was kept and filed with the *H*'s on the finder's bookshelf, picked up on occasion, and thumbed through quizzically. (*Ça veut dire* a-w-e-s-o-m-e?) I suppose the book could also just have been tossed—it was a slight paperback after all, weighty only to its owner.

* Hadley, Ernest Hemingway's first wife, lost all his early manuscripts (both the originals and carbon copies) on a train to Paris. She felt guilty about this for the rest of her life.

Of the many, many cherished things I have lost over the years—a leather-bound notebook filled to the brim with ideas: gone; a marionette puppet I crafted for my parents: gone; an entire suitcase at the airport: gone—that copy of *A Moveable Feast* is the only item I often think about and would very much like back. ■

If you know anything about my lost copy of
A Moveable Feast, text **Have clue**.

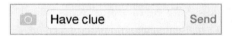

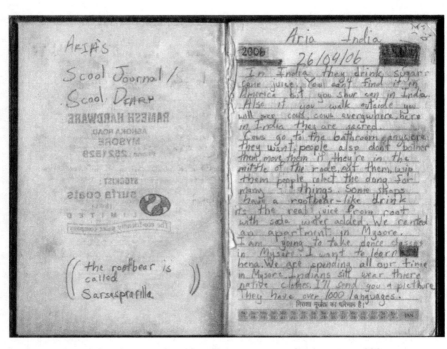

FIG. 1   I found this diary on the sidewalk in Mysore, India, in 2006. I'd like to return it to you, Aria.

I am looking out the hotel window. There are hot pink and fuchsia flowers as far as I can see. For no particular reason, I take a small step back.

An aproned woman hanging clothes on a laundry line across the way is unexpectedly added to my range of vision. I reflexively step forward to my initial spot, returning to the lush and uncluttered image. But as soon as I do, it washes over me that the version with the flowers and the woman and the drooping laundry line is just as—maybe even more—beautiful.

I step back again. ■

FIG. 1

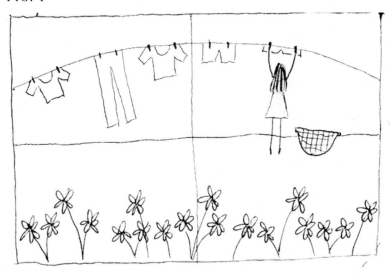

The author of the book I am reading (*Textbook Amy Krouse Rosenthal*)
asked me to tear out this page and give it to someone—
someone I know or someone who is a complete stranger.

I am choosing you.

She (Amy) orchestrated this as a simple way to bring us together—
three beings (you, me, her) who would most likely never otherwise
share a connection.

Perhaps this means absolutely nothing to you,
being handed a random piece of paper with a ragged edge.
But what if it happens to mean everything?

Either way, please know that on the afternoon of January 9, 2015,
the author was thinking about us
and imagining our exchange.

Signed _____   ___/___/_____   _____
          the reader   given to you on this day   location

Signed ___*Amy K*___   _1_/_9_/_15_   _Chicago_
          the author   thinking about us on this day   location

Social
Studies

There is an individual honey packet peeking out from under the passenger seat of my car. It's been there for months. The first time I spotted it, my hands were full, so I left it to throw out next time. Then the next time I was like, *Oh yeah, there's that lone little honey packet.* From that point on, I haven't been able to bring myself to discard it. It can't be that it's too much trouble—it involves reaching down and picking up a minuscule item. It can't be because I don't care about the cleanliness of my car—I keep it rather tidy. I can only conclude that, for some reason, I have become attached to the honey packet. ∎

My favorite Craigslist experience started with a simple posting: *I'll wish you luck in exchange for you wishing me luck.* The offer was sincere, not one bit silly or coy, but I wasn't sure how it would come across, how people would interpret it. But they totally got it. People emailed back asking for me to wish them luck on their divorce, luck with their new boss, luck finding a new job, luck finding an apartment. I asked them to please wish me luck with my children, and with my latest book. I had several meaningful and sweet email exchanges. Some time later—and you'd really have to be digging backward to have found my inital posting—I received what turned out to be the final email. *I don't know if you still need it, but I wanted to wish you the best of luck. You can do it.*

He asked for nothing in return. ■

(Text) Message in a Bottle

Text a short good luck message
for yourself
or someone else.
Every January 1st,
all messages will be
gathered, placed inside a bottle,
and tossed out to sea.
First, text **Bottle**.

| 📷 | Bottle | Send |

Two Stages of Life

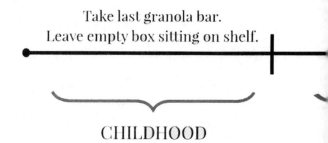

Take last granola bar.
Leave empty box sitting on shelf.

CHILDHOOD

Take last granola bar.
Throw out empty box.

ADULTHOOD

I had been toying with the idea of a minimalist wardrobe for nearly a decade. I always imagined that having a set daily uniform would feel fabulous and freeing. In hindsight, I'm not sure why I thought this; it's not like I'm well put-together—I spend about ten seconds getting ready every day. In any event, on one fittingly drab January 1st, I decided, enough thinking about the sartorial experiment. It was time to actually do it.

The rules I set for myself were these: I would wear gray pants and a solid black top. Because I like to wear casual, flippy dresses, it was deemed that plain black dresses would also be allowed. These permissible garments remained in my closet; I had a few of each—enough to get by and still be a clean person. Everything else was either given away or shoved into—I mean neatly folded and placed into—a black Hefty bag, which then camped out in my crawl space for fifty-two unfashionable weeks.

I didn't tell anyone except my family and a couple close friends about this endeavor. Why?

Because: weird.

Because: who cares.

Two, three months into the project I started having pangs of *uh-oh, this is miserable.* But there was no turning back. I knew I was in it for the long haul, both for my own follow-through reasons and also because teenage Paris was into it in a *that's-odd-and-I-would-for-sure-never-do-that-but-good-for-you-for-sticking-with-your-dumb-project* sort of way.

About six months in, on the eve of heading out of town for a book tour, I decided I was going to be naughty and cheat on my project. *It's perfect!* I thought. *Some people go away on business and cheat on their mates, and while that version isn't my thing, this wardrobe-cheating version is so my thing!* I rationalized my planned indiscretions by saying it was good fodder for my experiment. Oh, how I loved sneaking into the crawl space that night and grabbing one patterned dress after the other. It was, I believe, the first time I ever experienced feelings of euphoria while packing.

The first stop on my tour was Minneapolis. Our old babysitter, Emily, had moved there and showed up at the book signing with her adorable new baby. Of course I had to take some pictures to send to the kids. Two seconds later I got a text back from Paris.

> **What are u doing?!**

> **Why r u wearing that dress?!!!**

Busted. By a careless text. It was so comically cliché, even down to my quick, frantic reply: *I can explain!*

When I returned home from that trip, I had a few more months to go. Getting dressed was always easy but never pleasing. I trudged along to the finish line.

In the end, after twelve monotone months, the most illuminating thing was this: No one noticed. Not one single person ever said to me, *Amy, why are you wearing those same gray pants and black shirt every time I see you?* This information is equal parts humbling, depressing, and liberating.

I woke up on January 1st to the most glorious gift from Jason—a pair of bright yellow jeans hanging in the closet. ■

FIG.1   Gray pants

FIG.2   Black dress

11/24/2013

Subject:	wardrobe experiment
From:	brooke hummer
To:	amy krouse rosenthal
Date:	Sunday, November 24, 2013 11:53 AM

Dear Amy,

Having known about the project from beginning, it's true - I also imagined that you would discover depth and meaning from the project, that "fasting" from fashion would liberate you in some profound way.

And I assumed you would have TONS of insight to share with us!!! It's hilarious that the conclusions were so simple...No one noticed and it was tedious. I still think these revelations are profound. I actually think the piece is even funnier because the conclusion is so anticlimactic.

As an aside, I want to add that as one of the few who knew you were doing the project, there was never even one single moment when I noticed your clothing at all - meaning I never looked at you thinking, oh that old gray thing again, poor Amy and her project. Unless you mentioned your clothes - which you did sometimes, usually in the context of being sick of them - I never, ever registered what you were wearing, good or bad.

Since I am someone who always notices other people's cute clothes (and loves to have cute clothes), the lesson there for me is, we notice the good in those we love, not the bad. Maybe it's that we are all loved in spite of our clothes not because of them but we still love getting dressed up sometimes?

Clothing is a little like food. Everyone has to have it and so everyone has to have a "relationship" with food/clothes, sometimes complicated, sometimes obsessed, sometimes "who cares."

Brooke

https://us-mg7.mail.yahoo.com/neo/launch?.rand=dogala9916271088qq#019238253888

F I G . 1   Email from friend Brooke, who was with me on the January 1st conclusion of project

If you announce or demonstrate a fondness for a particular snack or treat in the company of an adoring and thoughtful family member, there is a good chance that they will instantly link it to you. The next time you are their guest, they will excitedly bring you by the arm over to the bowl/dish/tray that holds this favorite item of yours. You may or may not love the item as much as they think you do. Either way, the food association will likely continue for the rest of your life. ▪

PERSON	PERCEIVED LOVE OF WHICH FOOD?	BY WHICH FAMILY MEMBER(S)?	DOES PERSON ACTUALLY LOVE IT?
Jason	pistachio nuts	his mom	no
Brian	peanut M&M's	his mom	no
Miles	capers	his grandparents	no
Ruby	goat cheese	her Aunt Margie	yes
	beets	her dad	yes
	pumpkin pie	her mom	no
Me	potato chips	all	yes

FIG.1 Person-food associations

The same message kept popping up on the treadmill: *USER NOT DETECTED ON BELT.* I had to keep fiercely pressing some button. *I am right here! I am walking on the belt! I do so exist!* The machine elicited uncomfortable feelings in me. I felt inconsequential and ignored. ▪

Mundane Highs and Lows

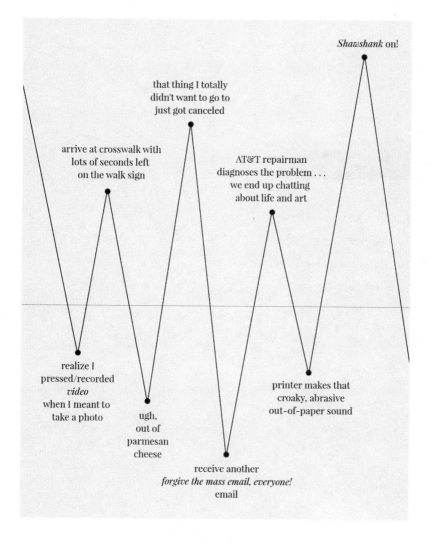

Short Answer

Noticing an older, hippie-ish-looking couple, Jason turned to me and said, *They definitely compost.*

compare *contrast*

Our waiter is kinda checking on us too much.

Where the heck is our waiter?

I think this is a story about the unsuspecting ripple-effect influence we have on one another. Or maybe it's a parable about trusting your instincts. It goes like this: A friend was telling us about being at an artists' retreat in California. The first day she spotted someone who had an uncanny resemblance to the comedian Andy Kaufman—something about his mannerisms and demeanor. She was sure he must hear this all the time, so she refrained from jostling him with the obvious. But after a couple more days, she could not shake the pull to approach him, and their conversation was revelatory. Did Andy K. Doppel-gänger hear this all the time? No, he did not; in fact, she was the first person to ever say this. *But funny you should say so*, he says, *because guess what?*—and this is the part where I imagine confetti being released from the ceiling—*Andy Kaufman's parents and my parents were best friends.* ∎

A college friend and her fiancé came to visit when Jason and I were first married. They stayed with us for one night. I'm pretty certain we had a fine time. But the one crisp, lingering memory is that we—Jason and I—somehow failed to provide them with pillows. It came up the next morning at breakfast. You could say we were just young and inexperienced hosts—both true—but that doesn't really cut it. When tending to the comfort of a houseguest, there are but a meager smattering of slumbering accessories to remember. And how could we possibly forget the most important one of all? Plus, I happen to have a deep affection for pillows. Pillows are the best. They were both jovial good sports—*We were FINE! We'll just remember to bring our own pillows next time!*—and we all *ha ha ha* had a good laugh. But I felt, and still feel, ashamed by such a bizarre and sloppy oversight. ∎

Resolutions of Bewilderments

BEWILDERMENT	EPIPHANY TIME DELAY	OH!	RESOLUTION
Did the reporter really just say that a new poem has been released? This is fantastic. Poetry is finally getting the attention it deserves.	a few seconds	Oh!	He said a new *poll* has just been released.
What is this I'm feeling while being administered the elementary school hearing test, listening for the beep, raising my right hand, left hand, right hand, left hand, left hand, left hand, right hand?	many years	Oh!	Dutiful. The word is dutiful.
Why is there a puppy yelling in the next aisle?	a minute or so	Oh!	Those are the wheels of a squeaky grocery cart.
What the heck, why is it actually impossible to put on my sandals?	several minutes	Oh!	The cobbler reattached the buckle completely backwards.
Why do we always end the school day by putting our chairs on top of our desks?	a couple decades	Oh!	It makes sweeping easier for the night-shift janitor.
Why am I so acutely annoyed by the way he drinks orange juice?	a few months	Oh!	This will not be a long-term relationship.
Why, after I blew out the candles and answered their question about my age, are my coworkers all throwing their heads back and muttering *23, 23, 23?*	25 years	Oh!	They see me as enviably young.

At the luncheon, Nora Ephron was the guest speaker. She was thoroughly charming, interesting, engaging. But I couldn't stop watching the waiter assigned to the table next to ours. The other servers were much younger, much more confident and agile. He was an older gentleman. He had a slow, subservient manner, as if always half expecting to be reprimanded by his manager. He was working hard. He dropped a knife at one point and it made a loud clink. He looked around nervously. I felt so bad for him. ∎

There was a time when I did not fully understand the concept, pervasiveness, and tentacles of sadness. I can point to the precise spot and moment I first had an inkling that the landscape around the bend was probably going to change—still vast and vastly beautiful but maybe with more parched patches than I was accustomed to. It was at a movie theater in Boston in the fall of my freshman year of college. One of the characters said, *I haven't met that many happy people in my life; how do they act?* It took some recalibrating in my mind and shifting in my seat to make sense of the line. *Aha,* I realized. *This character must not be unusual.* ■

UNIT 2

Usually I can figure out who Jason is talking to on the phone—by his phrasing, by his inflection, by his level of brevity. But he's really throwing me for a loop here. His responses are so unusual and confusing. With scrunched eyebrows, I keep mouthing to him:

Who is it?

Who is it? ■

I was reading *Interview* magazine. Looking at the table of contents, I knew I wanted to read two pieces: Billie Jean King interviewing Roger Federer, and Whoopi Goldberg interviewing Amy Sedaris. I began reading the first article. Somehow I totally tangled who was interviewing whom, even though I had just moments ago read the correct pairings, not to mention (of course) the clear connection between interviewer and interviewee. So I am reading the Federer interview and Whoopi (who is really Billie Jean King, but I'm thinking she is Whoopi) says, *Yeah, I remember I saw you at that big party before the US Open.* And I'm kind of intrigued—*Okay, cool, I didn't know Whoopi was so serious about tennis.* And on it goes like this for about half the interview, me being swept along by the Whoopi–Federer narrative. When it finally clicked back into place—*it's Billie Jean King, not Whoopi, interviewing Federer!*—I had to do a whole reset and was reluctant to part with the (non) reality I had unwittingly constructed. ■

You don't really see chubby symphony conductors. ■

You run into someone from elementary school, someone you haven't seen in forever. *How have you been, what have you been up to?!* they ask. There are many ways to come at this question, but considering your shared history—you were once prepubescent fort-makers together—there is really only one response: *What have I been up to? I'll tell you the biggest, craziest thing since I last saw you: A few humans tumbled out of my lady parts.* ∎

I was standing in front of the mirror. I dared myself to cut off my hair. I did it. Now I feel like I can do anything in the world. ■

About that past social transgression, that unflattering, face-flushing faux pas you imagine is being relentlessly snickered about in your absence, the one you've been replaying over and over in your mind—I'm not sure stressing about it is a great use of time. To wit, when I hadn't seen H. in a couple years, the very first thing he said—and I had no clue what he was talking about—was: *Amy, I want to apologize for eating all your pâté last time I saw you.* ■

defining word

small

1. I have been and have felt small for as long as I can remember. The kind of small that gets you immediately placed in the front for group photos. The kind of small that in order to retrieve things from cupboards requires slinging a knee onto the kitchen counter and boosting yourself up. In grade school I was called Krouse Mouse—affectionately, I think . . . At least I don't recall it feeling like a diss. Many of those childhood pals still greet me that way in person, in greeting cards, in texts.

2. I almost always have to get my pants shortened. I almost

never have to duck. A coach seat is perfectly roomy.

3. After it was clear we were kind of falling in love but before the meeting-of-the-parents, Jason's mom asked him to describe me. As the story goes, the first thing he said was, *Well, she's small.*

4. There was one period of my life where I actually felt tall, and that was when I towered over my young children. This was, um, short-lived.

5. When I started creating YouTube videos, I grappled with what term to use when asked. *Videographer* sounded like I filmed weddings. *Filmmaker* sounded like I thought I was all that. Finally I landed on just the right phrasing: I am a *tiny filmmaker*. Whether one interprets that as a person who makes tiny films or a tiny person who makes films, both are correct.

6. I wonder how it would feel to not have to crane my head upward when chatting at cocktail parties. I wonder how it would feel to be able to see no matter where I stood at the concert (and I wonder why no one has invented a concert snorkel, a periscope attached to sunglasses). I wonder if most people are familiar—though I am not—with the top of my head.

7. I sometimes get the sense that when readers meet me, there is a discrepancy between the me they imagined and the me who shows up. Perhaps they were expecting someone taller. Or maybe it's not a height thing at all—maybe they just thought I'd be younger, or be more of an airbrushed pretend person, or have a nicer coat. Even if I'm in the zone of what they were expecting, the prevailing sentiment still

might be: *Something's different here.* For example, *Oh, you got your hair cut*, I heard recently. I could tell by her tone that it wasn't a gleeful, girl-to-girl observation—her inflection didn't go up on the word *hair*—but rather a *you tampered with something that belongs to me* remark. So a few years ago I explored the idea of finding someone else to actually be a stand-in for me. I posted an ad, then held auditions with a waiting room and a snack table and everything. It was terribly fascinating, listening to people (men and women both) read from one of my books, trying to decipher who would be the best me. There were some excellent candidates, but in the end the project lost traction (for me) and I let it fizzle. I still keep in touch with one of the front-runners, though, an artist and swell chap who now resides in London. He would have been a great and tall me. ■

Matching

Perhaps we should get matching tattoos.

Send along an idea.

Make sure you are serious about this because I am.

How's that for author and reader bonded by ink.

First, text **Tattoo**.

SOCIAL STUDIES

G7   D   A

It is easy to fall in love with someone who passes the time at the airport gate strumming their guitar. ■

Aviation etiquette has evolved in such a way that it is no longer customary to thank our pilots for the flight. (Unless it's a long international flight—then the passengers, exhausted and giddy, break out into applause. I always love that.) We thank all the other travel-related transporters: cabdrivers, bus drivers, hotel shuttle drivers, rickshaw drivers. Yet we do not verbally acknowledge our gratitude to those who maneuver lumbering masses of aluminum through the sky and somehow manage to tippy-toe touch down with two grocery-cart-sized wheels. The flight attendants are clearly trained to thank us as we exit the aircraft, and so when I am rounding the corner and handed one of their courtesy thank-yous, I always toss it back like a hot potato—*Thank YOU*, I'll say, looking directly at the pilot. But the pilots never appear to care one way or the other. They just stand there, hunched in the cockpit entryway, relaxed like it was no big deal, waiting patiently for us to file out. ■

Jason and I were at a concert. While waiting for the headliners to take the stage, a camera was panning the audience, projecting people dancing on the big screen. The camera landed on a tall, gangly guy with a bopping mop of hair. When he saw himself on the screen, he kicked into high gear, dancing in an adorably enthusiastic and goofy way. He worked the crowd into a frenzy. A few seconds later the headliners walked on stage. The camera was still on him, and everyone had just erupted into full-on applause and woo-hoo-ing. You could tell by his expression that he believed the rousing applause was for the band. He will never know that it was really for him. ■

UNIT 2

Retention of Passing Comments

WHAT WAS SAID	HOW OFTEN I THINK ABOUT IT
When you see a stray popcorn kernel on the ground, you place one next to it so that it won't feel so lonely.	kind of a lot
You would stand on a chair and converse with the stuffed moose head.	not that often
You left me a voicemail that was a strange combination of estimating and being overly specific. (*Hey, it's about 7 minutes after 2:00.*)	with some regularity
One of your students needed winter boots but couldn't afford them. So you went to the store to buy a pair. There in the aisle you made small talk with a mother and her young son. You mentioned you were getting boots for your boot-less student. The mother said, *Here. Take my son's boots.* She insisted. What you remember most: the image of the boy walking away barefoot.	occasionally
When you woke up, for a moment you thought you were the moon.	quite a bit
You were so busy thinking about nothing.	every now and then, wistfully
I asked if you felt content most of the time. *Yes*, you said. *Isn't that terrible?*	often

Just look at us, all of us, quietly doing our thing and trying to matter. The earnestness is inspiring and heartbreaking at the same time. ■

More than half of the calls I receive from my dad are pocket calls. I've stopped telling him, because what is the point?

> ME: *Dad, you pocket dialed me again.*
> HIM: *I did?*

When I see his name pop up on my phone, I still always answer with a perky *Hi, Dad*. I have not yet defaulted to the stance that he is probably calling me unknowingly. It is only after a couple *Dad? Dad?*s followed by that distinct brand of garble (tunnel voice, crinkly static, whooshes of wind) that I all at once register, remember, and accept what's at hand. I'll try to make out a word or pin down a familiar sound just for the sport of it, but after a few undecipherable syllables I press *end call* and return to the matters of the day. There was one Saturday morning, however, where somehow his pocket call came in crystal clear. Almost immediately I could tell who he was with and what they were doing: He was with my mom and they were playing golf. I listened in for a minute but then hung up because it felt sneaky. About thirty seconds later my dad "called" me again; at this point I decided it was more than okay to eavesdrop—this was an unexpected gift and I was happy to receive it. I put my mom and dad—who have been married more than fifty years—on speakerphone, poured myself a cup of coffee, and took notes for an hour.

Their dialogue consisted almost entirely of sweet encouragements. *Nice shot! Very nice! Oh my, that's a beauty! Oh yeah, honey . . . lovely. What, honey? I know, honey. Absolutely perfect!* There was one bit of advice, gently delivered: *I think you took too long thinking about that last shot and lost your rhythm.* There were two other sounds I could make out in the background: the golf cart as they drove from hole to hole. And birds—every few minutes, I could hear birds. I like to think they were lovebirds. ■

When my life flashes before my eyes, I hope my subconscious turns out to be a skilled curator. It would be unfortunate to be stuck watching a montage of all the times I bent down to pick up those flimsy subscription cards that fall out of magazines. ∎

FIG.1

Being divided into groups has always played out the same for me, whether we're talking middle school or middle age. The leader eyeballs the room and either sections us off or instructs us to count off by threes: *All "ones" over there, "twos" over here . . .* First I will feel unsettled; I will be skeptical about these people in my group. I will look over at the other groups and conclude: *Yep, I've definitely got the bad group.* I'll accept my lot in life and then—because really, what other choice is there?—resign myself to the group. I will slowly but surely begin to enjoy, connect with, appreciate, and, ultimately, bond with my group. Now I just love my group. I got the best group. ∎

Matching

To be matched (via email) with two other readers,

go to **Match Me** at textbookamykr.com.

Perhaps the three of you will become dear, digital companions.

Or start a business.

Or end up vacationing together in the Caribbean. ∎

ART

For You, Me, and the Elephant in the Room
bowl, fifty-three peanuts (with shells on)
exhibited on kitchen table to coincide with guest's arrival
2015

Flyer

paper, black marker

exhibited on community bulletin boards

2015

Flyer (detail)

Self-Portrait (diptych)

pen on paper

2003

Send in your own self-portrait . . . a photo, drawing, painting, any medium at all.

It will then be added to the website's gallery of **Readers' Self-Portraits**.

First, text **Self portrait**.

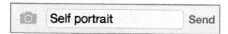

Existential Napkin

ink printed on disposable napkin

dispensed at local restaurant

1999

Just Add Daughter
photographs
outfits picked and laid out by daughter on
nights before preschool
2000

Book Jacket Jacket
book jackets from thirteen books
adhered to muslin, stitched with thread
April 2015

 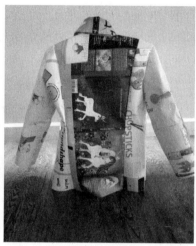

Venting to Black Hole

email intentionally sent to Postmaster Undeliverable address

August 2015

8/10/2015

Subject:	venting
From:	amy krouse rosenthal
To:	MAILER-DAEMON@yahoo.com
Date:	Monday, August 10, 2015 2:13 PM

Dear Postmaster Undeliverable,

I want you to know three things about the guy at the table next to me at Starbucks:

1. He just bought a pair of 36'' pants from Banana Republic.
2. He is doing business with a friend (her name is Karen) and he is concerned about this hurting their friendship.
3. He makes frequent calls and talks very loud.

Sincerely,
Amy

A Penny for Your Thoughts
thoughts taped to pennies
exhibited on sidewalks around Chicago
2015

Text on Pennies

Penny 1: I just learned the German word *fernweh*, sort of a cousin to wanderlust; it means "far-sickness, an ache for distance."

Penny 2: With the kids now all out of the house, I find myself having random, panicky, parenting thoughts such as: *Wait! Did I forget to teach them to look both ways even on a one-way street??!!*

Penny 3: If you ever meet Neil deGrasse Tyson, please tell him this anagram for his name: *Is N. astro legend? Yes!*

Penny 4: Driving along, I noticed a piece of chocolate cake in the middle of the road. When I think about it now, it feels like art.

Freezing Time: 7/13/2015 6:15pm
The Moment When I Was Walking Along the Lake
and Talking to My Son on the Phone
water taken from Lake Michigan, placed in baggie, frozen in ice cube tray

Freezing Time: 8/04/2015 10:00pm
The Moment When My Daughter and I Were Drinking Tea Together
on the Night Before She Left for College
tea taken from her glass, placed in baggie, frozen in ice cube tray

SCIENCE

THE RAINBOW EXPERIMENT

1. Look up at the sky.

2. Do you see a rainbow?
   If so, snap a photo.

3. Now text **Rainbow.**

   You will then be prompted to send the photo.

4. Your rainbow and its location will be posted on the
   Live Rainbow Feed at textbookamykr.com.

5. Rainbow posts will remain live for one day. So at any given
   moment, we will be able to see where in the world there are
   rainbows.

6. After the one day, each rainbow will be moved to the
   Permanent Archive of Beautiful Ephemera.

THE PRIVATE INVESTIGATOR EXPERIMENT

1. Fall and stay in love.

2. Remain loyal.

3. Sometime later, hire a private investigator who specializes in
   infidelity work. Hire this private investigator over the phone;
   do not meet in person.

4. Email photos of your beloved to the private investigator.

5. Tell the private investigator that you know for certain that your
   beloved will be with the "other person" at such and such a time at
   such and such a place, and that you want photos.

6. Arrive at that place, at that time, with your beloved.

7. This place might be your favorite restaurant. Or a park bench.
   Or even just your home.

8. Wherever it is, make sure the two of you are easily visible to
   the private investigator (who will be staked out nearby—maybe
   across the street, or hiding in a bush). If you are at a restaurant,
   for example, sit at a window table. If at home, maybe hold hands
   on your front porch, or embrace one another by a large window.

9. The private investigator will proceed to take long-lens,
   black-and-white photographs of the two (of you).

10. When you receive the photos, frame them for your home.

11. Title the series *Caught in the Act of Monogamy*.

THE PIÑATA EXPERIMENT

1. Procure a candy-filled piñata.

2. Hang this candy-filled piñata in a tree near a baseball field.

3. Affix a brief clarifying note next to the piñata that says, *Yes, this is for you.*

4. Sit back and wait for some baseball players (or Little Leaguers) to discover the piñata.

5. See how long it takes them to realize, *Hey, the perfect item for whacking this thing open is in our possession!* and watch as they gleefully have at it.

THE SHORT, COLLECTIVE BIOGRAPHY EXPERIMENT*

* Short, Collective Biography was originally launched as a collaboration between conceptual artist Lenka Clayton and myself at TEDActive 2015.

1. Gather between six and twelve people around a table, ideally over dinner.

2. The group can consist of good friends, individuals you are meeting for the first time, or any combination thereof.

3. Someone happily agrees to be a notetaker.

4. Through conversation, endeavor to find a collection of autobiographical statements that are equally true for each and every member of the group.

5. While it may begin with one person tossing out questions ("Does everyone like flannel?"), soon enough everyone will be chiming in, energy will escalate, and questions will bounce around in pinball fashion.

6. Maybe you will do this for 30 minutes. Maybe for a couple of hours. You'll know when to wrap it up.

7. Assemble your statements.

8. Call it your Short, Collective Biography.

I was born in the 20th century in the United States of America east of the Mississippi.

I have, at one point or another, been to New York City, dipped my toes in the Atlantic, owned a pet, and had an awkward autocorrect experience.

I have seen a full moon.

I have cried at a movie, messed up the lyrics of a song, am scared of death, and have burned toast.

I've started something that I did not finish, and mistakenly shrunk something in the wash.

I have forced myself to hydrate, gotten a scar, gotten a bad haircut, and said something that I've regretted.

I have never been followed by the paparazzi.

I have read *Green Eggs and Ham*, stayed up on an election night, walked in the rain, played on an Etch a Sketch, and watched at least half of *The Sound of Music*.

I have blushed, fallen in love, and pulled a pebble from my shoe.

FIG. 1 The Short, Collective Biography of Diane Bond, Emily RK Chester, Teri Cicurel, Jim Clark, Ann Kim, Krista Varsbergs, and Amy K.R. Created over dinner on Saturday night, August 15, 2015. Imagine it read by all seven people in unison.

THE COUCH EXPERIMENT

1. Start a family.

2. On a lazy Sunday morning shortly after your first child is born, take a family photo on the couch.

3. Put this first photo, and all subsequent photos, in a small album labeled *Couch Pictures*.

4. Repeat one or two Sundays a year, or whenever you happen to think of it.

5. When your children are preteens, there will be some nonsense complaints about doing the Couch Picture. Pay no attention. Proceed as normal.

6. Observe how one day you have an album full of Couch Pictures.

7. On the first Sunday after your last child leaves for college, take a Couch Picture with your mate, just the two of you.

8. When it occurs to you that removing the *c* from the word *couch* is more like it, do not actually label it as such. Proceed as normal.

THE APRIL 29TH EXPERIMENT

1. On 4/29 at 4:29pm, text someone *I love you*. This is what I would like for my birthday each year.

MIDTERM ESSAY

If it is wonderful, splendid, remarkable—a view outside a window, a lit-up fountain at night, that fig-chorizo appetizer—I am compelled to seek some sort of saturation point, to listen/stare/savor on a loop, to greedily keep at it until I've absorbed, absconded with, and drained it of all its magic. Invariably, I will have to move on before I have had enough. My first word was *more*. It may very well be my last.

***

About my midlife crisis. I did not get a sports car (staying with minivan). I did not run off with the ski instructor (staying with mate). I did not go on a cruise (staying at home).

But here is what I did get: weepy, chronically weepy.

I wouldn't describe the origin of my tears as *Boo-hoo, I'm so old,* but more, *Oh my, here I am, living, and I would like to keep on living, preferably perpetually.*

I would like to avoid, for as long as humanly possible, being pronounced dead and just keep being pronounced *AY-mee KROWSS ROH-zihn-THAHL*. I would like to say to that tomorrowless day (the one day that coyly begins

like any other but then ends—so nonchalantly! so dis-
missively! so boorishly!—without me in it), *STAY AWAY!*

But even if I were crowned life-expectantly average by
an optimistic actuary, the hourglass is now, at most,
half empty.

And so it was, everything around me had a bittersweet
sheen to it; moments were dramatically stamped FLEET-
ING and TRANSIENT as I roamed about. A simple exchange
between my son and me, for example, felt epic in its
beauty and poignancy; all that happened was that he
tapped on his bedroom window, I looked up at him from
the sidewalk below, and he waved.

I choked up at a Park District ice-skating show when
the girls did their synchronized straddle leaps just
as Irene Cara screams *FAME!* Something about the sin-
cerity of it all: the matching polyester costumes and
well-rehearsed jump in the air; the song itself, a
mighty combination of touching and kitsch. And I didn't
even have a kid in the show.

I lost it when my daughter excitedly asked me to quick
come outside, watch this: *See how much faster my new
sneakers make me run?*

I didn't exactly have a midlife crisis. I had a midlife
cry-bliss.

If one is generously contracted 80 years, that amounts to 29,220 days on Earth. Playing that out, how many more times then, really, do I get to look at a tree? 12,395? There has to be an exact number. Let's just say it is 12,395. Absolutely, that is a lot, but it is not infinite, and anything less than infinite seems too measly a number and is not satisfactory. Also, I would like to stare at my kids a few million more times. I could stare at them a few million more times easy.

Tell me:

How many more times do I get to cut an apple?

How many more times will I put on my shoes? Kiss my mother? Use an ATM?

How many more times do I get to toss the salad and ask *How much longer 'til the chicken's ready?* as Jason pokes at it on the grill? How many more times do I get to lift my head from the pillow to see what time it is? Run inside after getting drenched in the rain? Look for the Ping-Pong ball? Check my email? Text <3 to the kids? Catch a whiff of jasmine? Use a straw?

***

I have this vivid pictorial memory of being 9 years old, sitting on the sidewalk by my house and thinking, *There is nothing special about what I am doing right now, but I want to remember this moment, perfectly intact, for the rest of my life.*

I no longer remember the fine print of it—like what I was wearing, where my siblings were, if there were worms on the sidewalk—but I have a carefully preserved recollection of the certainty of my mission, of sitting there on that suburban subdivision sidewalk, feeling adamant about carrying the moment with me into old age. I swear I feel like I could just plop down on the curb next to that girl, she seems so close.

Hi there, 9-year-old me. Can you believe it? Here I am, that middle-aged me you imagined. And here we are together. And here is that moment, just like you wanted.

Yes. And what about the very old and very gray 80-year-old us? Is she coming?

I believe so. I hope so. Let's sit and wait. I have a feeling she will be here in no time. ∎

ROMANCE
LANGUAGE

CHARACTERS

Ana

Ana's mother Fran

Ana's best friend Peter

Ana's paternal grandmother Gram

Ana's dead father Frank

PRESENT TENSE

Ana & Peter:
14 years old
best friends since kindergarten

Ana calls him Re-Pete:
because he stutters

She also calls him Petep:
so they can both have
palindromic names

Gram has always called him
Sweet Pete:
because he is

PAST TENSE

In kindergarten, Fran nicknamed the two of
them Ampersand

On account of them having met in a sandbox

On account of them always
being together

PAST TENSE

Frank was an architect

He died unexpectedly and instantly from a
brain aneurysm

Ana was 12

Frank was 42

People who didn't know Frank well
said he died in the prime of his life

People who knew him would
never say that

Frank always said
Every day is the prime of your life

PRESENT TENSE

Ana and Gram are having lunch at their
favorite sushi place

They are sipping miso soup,
talking about Frank

As they often do, they begin doodling
anagrams on their napkins

They enjoy referring to themselves as
AnaGram

Gram writes: *I'm sad*

Ana's anagram response: *Is mad*

Ana writes: *Miss you so much*

They play around with this for a while

Gram puts a dash of soy sauce in both of their
miso soups

She shows Ana her anagram response:

us = miso soy chum

They clink bowls

PRESENT TENSE

Ana has a dream about her dead father

In the dream she runs into him at their
favorite deli

She can't believe it—
he's not dead after all

He clarifies that he is indeed dead but was
allowed to come back for a single day

Ana is ecstatic but panicked—
she feels they're wasting time at the deli

She insists they hurry home

Her father first wants to eat a
sandwich together

In this way it can just be a
regular day

Ana starts crying

You lied to me!

You said you would love me forever & always,
but you died!

The deli-counter man calls his number

27!

Instead of giving the deli-counter man
the paper ticket, her father puts it in Ana's hand

This ticket is for you, Ana.

It says everything.

He kisses her hand holding the 27 ticket

Ana wakes up

She is still crying

PRESENT TENSE

Ana shares "the 27 dream" with her mother

She shares the dream with Pete

She shares the dream with Gram

She begins having "the 27 dream" regularly

PAST TENSE

Ana and Pete were in 5th grade

Classmates were teasing Pete at recess about his
stuttering

Ana stood up for him

Back in class later,
they learned about Venn diagrams

Pete passed Ana a note

It was a Venn diagram

In the left circle he wrote
th-th-thank

In the right circle he wrote
y-y-y-you

In the overlapping center he wrote
from your best friend

She tacked this "sweet Venn thank-you" on her bedroom wall

It has been there ever since

PAST TENSE

Frank and 7-year-old Ana sat at
the dining room table

They were looking at architectural drawings for
their new dream house

Ana asked why it was taking so long to build
the house

Frank told her a year was actually rather fast

He showed her a photo of a house that took
22 years to build

It was the Taj Mahal

He told her the (true) story of the 17th-century
emperor whose beloved wife died

The emperor became despondent and had a
palace built to match the size of his grief

The story upset Ana

Frank made up a happier epilogue:

He told her that after the Taj Mahal was
completed, the emperor fell in love again!

The first time the emperor kissed his new love
it was at sunset in front of the palace

The moment they kissed it was as if lightning
struck his heart

He immediately knew their love
was everlasting

Ever since, through the ages, couples from all
over the world have journeyed to the Taj Mahal

They kiss at sunset

If lightning strikes their hearts,
they know their love is everlasting

Frank concluded the tale by sharing the
"famous poem" (made up on the spot)
about this legend:

> *Kiss under a dimming sun*
> *In front of the Taj Mahal*
> *And if thy heart lights up*
> *Yours is the truest love of all*

PAST TENSE

It was the night Fran and Frank first met

They were at a party

Hi, I'm Fran.

Fran is it? Well, that's cool.

And why is that cool?

Because based on our names alone,
it seems I complete you.

He reached to shake her hand:

Hello, Fran,
I'm Frank.

PAST TENSE

Frank handed Fran a ring

It was cobalt

Even more than gold, cobalt is the element of
enduring strength

FUTURE TENSE

Ana & Pete will decipher "the 27 dream"

They will discover that the ampersand was
originally the 27th letter in the English alphabet

They will discover that the atomic number
of cobalt is 27

They will discover there are 27 bones
in the human hand

They will discover that the largest prime
number ever calculated is 17,425,170 digits
long; those digits add up to 27

They will discover an anagram for
twenty seven = sweet Venn ty
(sweet Venn thank-you)

They will discover that there are two major
cities on earth with a latitude of 27 degrees:

Tampa, Florida

Agra, India

Tampa, Florida—
the place in the world where lightning strikes most

Agra, India—
home to the Taj Mahal

FUTURE PERFECT

Ana and Pete will have turned 27

They will have ventured to Agra, India

They will have stood in front of the Taj Mahal
under a dimming sun

Pete will have taken a cobalt ring from his pocket

He will have asked for her hand

He will have given her a piece of paper

It will have been something he realized years ago

He will have been waiting all this time to share it

Anagram for the word anagram:

Agra man

Ana, I'm your Agra man. ∎

HISTORY

Fall 2002

I am thinking good and hard about trying to turn my notes (what will eventually become *Encyclopedia of an Ordinary Life*) into some kind of a novel. It seems like that is what I am supposed to do: Get serious and tackle fiction already. Why be so hopelessly fixated on the truth, always telling it exactly like I see it, like I feel it against my skin? Alas, sitting in a room with all these scattered notes, observations, and word chunks, and trying to weave them into a made-up story (what story?) gives me heart palpitations and only further amplifies my shortcomings and nonfiction predilection.

January 2003

It occurs to me: What if I dump all the scattered notes, observations, and word chunks into the lap(top) of a fiction writer? A fiction writer with a penchant for collaborative, uncompensated experimentation. A fiction writer who would not find it tiresome or pointless to concoct an imaginary, truth-sprinkled version to live alongside the truth-truth version.

Spring 2003

A fiction writer pal—whose debut novel is in the works and who has no clue he will soon become a colossal, international success—says yes. He swiftly pens a robust tale involving my third-grade teacher, Katie Holmes, and Birmingham, Alabama. It is like a foreign edition, only the translation in this case is from English nonfiction to English fiction.

To read the short story,
text **Robust tale**.

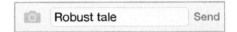

Summer 2003

I am at a coffeehouse working on the first draft of *Encyclopedia of an Ordinary Life*. I write exactly what I see, how I feel it against my skin:

There is a single purple flower a couple feet from where I am sitting. I am feeling poorly dressed and missing my long hair. I am at Café De Lucca in Bucktown, and there is a purple flower—that's how I would define this moment. And you, your moment? Where are you at this moment? E-mail me and tell me. If you are the hundredth person to do so, I will bake you a pie and FedEx it to you. You will have to trust me on this.

Summer 2004

Page 167 is designed.

> ## PURPLE FLOWER
>
> There is a single purple flower a couple feet from where I am sitting. I am feeling poorly dressed and missing my long hair. I am at Café De Lucca in Bucktown, and there is a purple flower—that's how I would define this moment. And you, your moment? Where are you at this moment? E-mail me and tell me. If you are the hundredth person to do so, I will bake you a pie and FedEx it to you. You will have to trust me on this.
>
> 167

Early January 2005

Encyclopedia of an Ordinary Life is published.

Mid-January 2005

The hundredth email comes in. I bake and FedEx a pecan pie to a Mr. Evans of Orlando, Florida.

End of January 2005

Mr. Evans confirms arrival and imminent consumption of pie.

Early February 2006

The paperback edition is published and the pie offer goes into effect for the second time.

Mid-February 2006

Ms. Hamilton submits the hundredth email. As it happens, Ms. Hamilton is also from Orlando, Florida, though no relation or connection to Mr. Evans at all.

January 2005–Present

I read countless purple flower moments, from people of all ages, from all over the world. People write about grand things (love, loss) and wee things (it's raining, there's a grape on the floor). Sometimes an email dialogue sprouts, and then a friendship.

This privileged peek into humanity brings to mind the scene in Wim Wenders's movie *Wings of Desire* where the angel—in the form of a man riding the subway—scans the thoughts of his fellow passengers, tuning into their quotidian worries, existential ruminations, and simple, serene contentments.

Winter 2013

Insights about pie seekers are summarized as a pie chart.

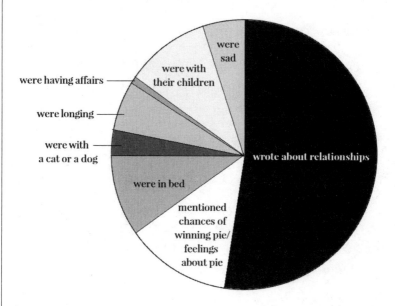

Summer 2015

I gather half a dozen moments to create the following purple flower arrangement.

Here is how

I would define the moment I was in when I
read the Purple Flower Moment in your book: In spite
of wearing sweats and socks to bed, I am freezing. I usually
sleep with nothing on, but I can't do that here—the ventilation is
too cold and blows too strong in the nine-man berthing space of this
submarine. As I am thinking of how to describe this to you, I know that
I have to tell you that this bunk (or rack, as we call it) has essentially the
same interior dimensions as a coffin. That strikes me as near perfect.
I am punching holes in the ocean, far beneath the surface, buried
beneath the waves and cold, numb from the freezing wind,
feeling next to nothing, except, as I drop the open book
on top of me, incredibly alive, as the purple flower

falls to my breast.

I'm missing my mom,

who passed away a little over a year ago.
Everywhere I go, I see little old ladies who might have
reminded me of her, except they're either painted with
"surprise" eyebrows, drive a purple Caddy, or grumble to
complete strangers about their aching joints. Except for the lady
in produce, whose wispy white hair and brown eyes make my
heart beat faster for a moment. I coax her into a conversation
about tomatoes-on-the-vine, and then we part. I watch her
round the corner into the soup aisle, and a lump catches
in my throat. As if on cue, she turns back.
And she smiles. She'll never know

what a gift that was.

I am home alone,

in bed, with a purring cat at my side,
wondering if my biopsy results will confirm
that I have breast cancer. I think that if I do, I am
going to send everyone I know a copy of a picture of
me taken a few summers ago, on a nude beach
in a nature preserve, surrounded by cows,
on the pure white sand of Majorca, Spain;
because my right boob sure does
look fab in this picture . . .

I am in Togo.

West Africa. At this exact moment
(earlier recorded in journal, copied now),
I am lying on my bed in a concrete bedroom
with one window. There is sweat soaking my
sheets, my hair is dirty (haven't had the
energy to wash it in 3 days), but I am
smiling because I love my life as
a Peace Corps volunteer.

I was at a café

in Roseville, California, reading
your book over a cup of coffee. I paused
after reading the selection and smiled while
looking up. This nice-looking younger
woman smiled at me. I am a 61-year-old
man and not too many younger women
smile at me these days.
Thank you.

I am in a waiting room

in a hospital gown next to an irate woman
who is tired of waiting for her ultrasound results.
I, luckily, brought this book with me to my doctor's
appointment. It really helped take my mind off my impending
miscarriage. It is a moment I won't forget. Reading about the
purple flower, thinking about losing a tiny baby, and knowing
there is always hope after tragedy. On my way home from
the ultrasound, I was telling my husband that I thought
maybe this would be the last time we try to have a
baby, when I looked up and read the license
plate in front of me. It read,
TRYAGAN.

This moment now.

Once again I must ask:

Where are you?

How would you describe this moment now?

If yours is the hundredth submission,

I will bake and FedEx you a pie.

To submit your moment

(and/or to view those from other readers),

go to **Purple Flower Moments** at textbookamykr.com.

There's a spot for the pie winner front and center.

MUSIC

"The music is not in the notes,

UNIT 7

but in the silence between." ■

(This quote has been attributed to both Wolfgang Amadeus Mozart and Claude Debussy.)

MATH

September 16th is
the most common   +
birthday in the world

On average, a baby's
first word is spoken   =
at 12 months of age

September 16th is the day of the year when
the most humans utter their very first word

(patience + silence) × coffee =

Poetry

(patience + silence) × beer =

Fishing

I am filling up
at the gas station

\+

My sons are in the
backseat listening
to music

\+

My daughter runs
inside to get   =
cough drops

物の哀れ A Japanese term (pronounced *mo-noh noh ah-WAH-ray*) meaning an awareness of the imperma-nence of all things and a wistful, gentle sadness at their passing

10 toes   +   1 pair of sandals
revealing the   =
first two toes on each foot

94% chance I touched up the peeking-out toes with
nail polish right after putting on aforementioned
sandals and just before seeing you

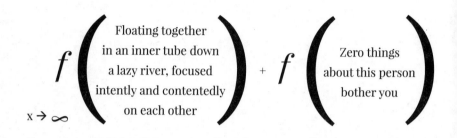

$$\lim_{x \to \infty} f \left(\begin{array}{c} \text{Floating together} \\ \text{in an inner tube down} \\ \text{a lazy river, focused} \\ \text{intently and contentedly} \\ \text{on each other} \end{array} \right) + f \left(\begin{array}{c} \text{Zero things} \\ \text{about this person} \\ \text{bother you} \end{array} \right) =$$

Everything in your blurry periphery looks like the hyper-colorful board of Candy Land.

Falling in love

$8/08/08 + 9/09/09 + 10/10/10 + 11/11/11 + 12/12/12 =$

Text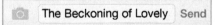

7:45   40   +   turn page upside down   =

MATH

Oh shit

son + onions =

$$\left(\quad \begin{array}{l}\text{1 bag frozen} \\ \text{peas, cooked}\end{array} \quad + \quad \begin{array}{l}\text{Small bunch} \\ \text{of cilantro}\end{array} \quad + \quad \text{3 Tbs tahini} \quad + \quad \text{2 cloves garlic} \quad +\right.$$

$$\text{Touch of olive oil} \overline{)^{\text{Salt to taste}}} \div \text{Cuisinart} =$$

Rosenthal House Special Pea Dip

Backpack at feet   +   Notebook in lap   +   Sugar wrappers on tray table   +   Fingertips prickly with the salt of mixed nuts   +

Music pouring   +   A magnificent,   =
through headphones   wide-awake sun bursting
                            through a too-small window

That moment on the plane

radiant   +   redolent   +   gorgeous   +   melancholy   +

patina + rhapsody + calm =

Words I kept trying to find a home for in this book

Nothing >

Love

LANGUAGE
ARTS

I kept a vocabulary journal when I was 23. It was the year I moved to San Francisco for my first job. I filled the journal with the (many) words I came across in books and in the workplace that I either needed clarity on or just flat out did not know. I walked to work almost every day that year—it was 30 minutes from my tiny studio apartment to the office—and I used that time to study the definitions. I found it to be an enjoyable and rewarding routine, tackling what felt to me like big words and big hills. Just as each word had its own definition, each hill had its own thing: Atop one was the park where older Chinese women in slow motion and loose clothing practiced Tai Chi; one was the "walk up backward" hill, something I forced myself to do, heeding the advice of an opinionated, physically fit friend. I'd arrive at work each morning flushed, a tad breathy, and armed with a new word or two to take out for a spin if I was feeling conversationally brave. Many of the people I spent time with that year are forever equated with the vocabulary word they taught me just by using it in my presence. Coworker Peter = *sprightly*. Boss Jeff = *time-honored*. Coworker Betsy = *industrious*. Over the years, the pages of the journal have aged and softened along with me. ∎

FIG. 1

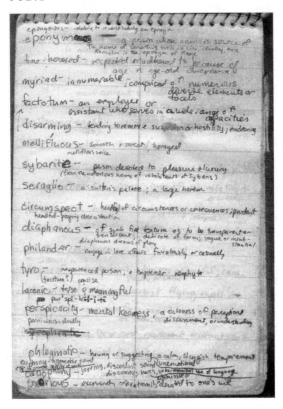

For a 7-minute audio recording of me reading words and definitions
verbatim from the journal, text **Vocabulary**.

Perhaps you will study these words on the way to your office too.

The *I* fell off the sign on the storefront stoop. It now spelled *NO SITTING ON STA RS*. But dang, wouldn't that be the best place of all to sit? ■

I dreamt I was at an exhibit where all the art was hung close to the ground. We were instructed to move through the gallery on our knees. Not only was this the most natural way to view the art (continuously bending down would be uncomfortable), but—and this was really the whole point—being on our knees dictated the pace. The show was called *Low and Slow*. ■

FIG. 1

The same five letters can be rearranged to express my daily sense of—and relationship to—time. First from the viewpoint of childhood, then young adulthood, and now, the present.

ACRES of it

CARES about it

RACES against it ∎

In 2001, I recorded the poet Kenneth Koch in his Upper East Side apartment reading his poem (one of my all-time favorites) "You Want a Social Life, With Friends." I used my trusty, turn-of-the-century RadioShack tape recorder, which explains the sound quality, but I actually like the crackling and soundprooflessness. He was an impeccable, flawless reader, and we finished in two or three takes. Though he had been reluctant to agree to our session, once under way, he was a gracious, charismatic host. He had set up a tray for us with glasses of grapefruit juice. Fitting, because our encounter proved to be bittersweet; Mr. Koch died a year later. The recording is one of his very last. ■

FIG.1

YOU WANT A SOCIAL LIFE, WITH FRIENDS

You want a social life, with friends,
A passionate love life as well
To work hard every day. What's true
Is of these three you may have two
And two can pay you dividends
But never may have three

There isn't time enough, my friends—
Though dawn begins, yet midnight ends—
To find the time to have love, work, and friends.
Michelangelo had feeling
For Vittoria and Ceiling
But did he go to parties at day's end?

Homer nightly went to banquets
Wrote all day but had no lockets
Bright with pictures of his Girl.
I know one who loves and parties
And has done so since his thirties
But writes hardly anything at all.

Poem by Kenneth Koch

Text **Koch**
to hear his one-minute recording.

compare **contrast**

YOU GRATE
YOU GREAT

WE ARE ALONE
WE ARE ALL ONE

WRITING
WRITHING

For the first decade of my life, I could not fathom what it would be like to have anything to say to people. I could not imagine ever speaking in (what I would later learn were called) declarative sentences. Adults—everyone in those days was an adult, even teenagers—seemed to "get" life. This rendered them wondrously skilled at stitching together non-interrogative utterances. They were able to offer comments, opinions, and explanations. I was chronically baffled, a cascade of questions spilling out of me at every turn:

Why is that lady doing that?
Where do towels come from?
Who actually makes towels?
What is going on in that tall building over there?
What is the man on the news even saying?
What happens if I shake this?

My plight (forever, I was certain) was to just figure out what the heck was going on with everyone everything everywhere. ■

I was texting with someone who had just lost her father. I was about to send the words *my phone is dying* but caught myself. This typically innocuous phrase suddenly felt jarring, sharp, insensitive. Choosing clunky over colloquial, I texted her *power running out!* ∎

Word Frequency in My Text Messages

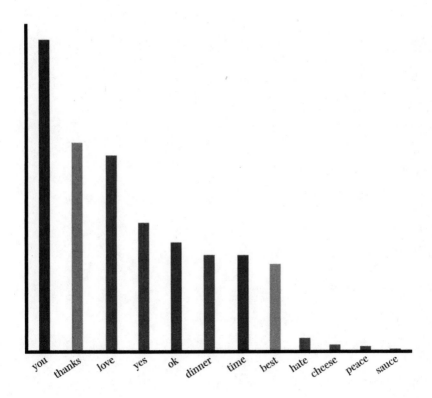

Because I also write children's books, there is a curious thing that transpires when people ask me about my work. I am often clarifying that I also write for adults, but saying *adult books* makes it sound like I write lewd porn-y stuff. The only viable solution so far seems to be saying I write *grown-up books*. But even that sounds wrong, and somehow infantilizing, like calling underwear *big-girl underpants.* ∎

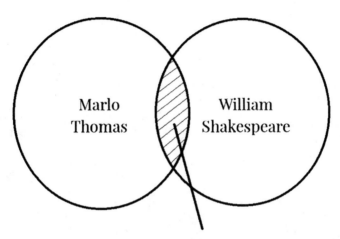

Free to Be, or Not to Be

The Bar Bar Graph

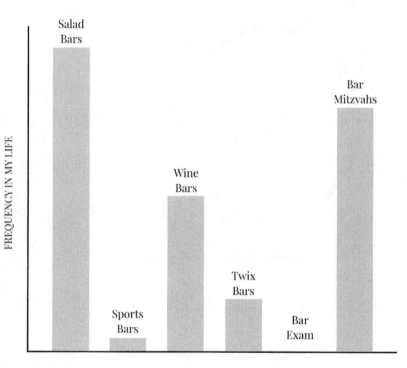

The Bracket Bracket

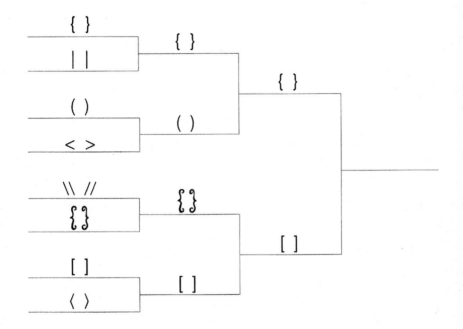

Text which bracket you deem the winner,

Curly or **Straight**.

Results regularly updated at textbookamykr.com.

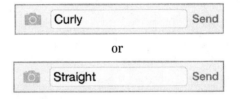

Really, what punctuation is one supposed to use?

_____ died.

_____ died!

_____ died . . .

Death demands its own designated punctuation mark.
Maybe:

_____ died /

It is a dividing line / everything on this side is different. ∎

I opened the kitchen drawer and announced, *We sure do have a plethora of ramekins!* It struck me as a peculiar yet accurate cluster of words. It hung in the air . . . like mini, domestic skywriting. I wondered how it would sound in other languages. ∎

FIG. 1

LANGUAGE	TRANSLATION
English	*We sure do have a plethora of ramekins!*
Spanish	*¡Estamos seguros que tenemos suficientes trastecitos!*
French	*Nous avons vraiment une pléthore de ramequins!*
Italian	*Abbiamo sicuramente una pletora di pirottini!*
German	*Natürlich haben wir ausreichend Aufflaufförmchen!*
Russian	*Да, у нас огромное количество горшочков!*
Mandarin Chinese	*我們當然有超多的烤布丁盅！*

Textbook rental,
Same-day delivery

Would you like me to show up at your door by day's end?

Perhaps you need a sous chef for your dinner party.

Or you'd like me to be the tail in your citywide bunny hop.

Send an idea that would prompt me to run upstairs, pack my bags,

and race to the airport.

I've always wanted to do something dramatic like this.

First, text **Amy rental**.

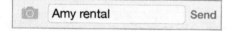

defining word

writer

1. I did not always know I wanted to be a writer. But I have always loved words. I have always loved the alphabet. When Justin was four, he asked, *What does it mean to be a writer?* I gave him a long, rambling answer. He thought about it for a moment and said, *So basically, you try to use all the letters?*

2. The word *literature* enters the room with its nose in the air. But get it in a corner, ask the right questions, and it will reluctantly fess up to its humble origins. *It hails from the Latin* litterae, you whisper

in your date's ear. *It puts on a
big act, but it literally just means
"things made of letters."*

3. I was enamored of typing
from the moment it was first
introduced to us in junior
high. The act of typing is a
happy, comfortable thing for
me. My fingers feel at home on
a keyboard, left hand resting
atop *a-s-d-f*, right hand on
j-k-l-semicolon. I like the
cursor blinking, the coffee
drinking, the sitting thinking.

4. I think it is a strength,
feeling tenderly about the nuts
and bolts and tools of one's
trade. But maybe it's not so
much a strength, more like
an indicator—strength implies
that I had some role in it, and
I don't believe I did; I was
simply born with a fondness
for letters and language, and
was predisposed to enjoy
playing around with them and

it. There is this anecdote from Annie Dillard: A painter was asked why he became a painter. He replied, *Because I love the smell of paint.*

5. As far as job titles go, *wordsmith* sounds nice to me—plain and simple and straightforward, yet still alluding to a mastered craft. It harkens back to other livelihood labels like *blacksmith* and *metalsmith*, smudgy-hand tinkerers us all.

6. I like that my first name happens to be the most symmetric name in the English language—first letter of the alphabet, exact middle letter of the alphabet, second-to-last letter of the alphabet. As far as I know, there is no such name as *Amz*.

7. I am an alphabetical-order junkie. Love using it, love spotting it. I was pleased to notice, decades after the fact,

that my siblings and I were named (not consciously) in a very spot-on kind of alphabetical order: close-in-age Amy and Beth, then a four-year gap, then close-in-age Joe and Katie. And now that I think about it, there is alphabetical precision to the names of my own offspring as well: exactly two years and two letters between each child: Justin, Miles, Paris.

8. It can neither be concealed nor overstated: These types of things genuinely interest and delight me. One small wordplay discovery—say, figuring out that an anagram for *maker* is *me, AKR*—will make my whole day.

9. Apparently the rules are that a sentence can't come right out and tell its writer what it is or wants to be, so the sentence gives the writer little clues, charade-style. The writer just

keeps churning/blurting things out, groping at the answer, trying out every possible assemblage. *It's a sentence about a man! It's a sentence about a woman! About a house? It's a long sentence. It's a short sentence? It's a sentence connected to another sentence by an ellipsis! Three syllables, first syllable starts with* L. *Um . . .* luminous! *Oh, second syllable starts with an* L. Alacrity? *The sentence is elegant and light! The sentence has something to do with a pear? Forget it, I have no idea. Start over.*

10. The question at the onset is always: What can the writer give the reader that they have not already received elsewhere? There are all those other books that have said all the things. And even if a writer manages to push out a magnum opus, you know what can happen? A reader may get in bed, flip open said magnum opus, and use a

few sentences as a handy exit ramp out of their day, letting the words pile up on their eyelids (*word, word, word, word, word, word, word, word, word*) until that reader succumbs to their weight and slips into sleep.

11. I like writing in the afternoon. The morning is the warm-up period. I can sometimes trick myself into a few sentences by standing at the counter eating a yogurt next to my laptop, which just happens to be open. But for the real thing, I need to sit down, feel the day's edges rub up against me, touch the afternoon with my left hand and impending evening with my right.

12. Why do I write? Because I can't not. There are other reasons (*recognition, money, mortality, job duty*), but they

are mere quarter notes on the staff, while *can't not* is the ever-present, fluttering, harmonious trill:

can't $_{not}$ can't $_{not}$ can't $_{not}$ can't $_{not}$

can't $_{not}$ can't $_{not}$ can't $_{not}$ can't $_{not}$

I (want to) believe that if I were cut off from the outside world and confined, indefinitely, to a small white room, I would still write. If, in that bare box of a room (I can't stand it—in my mind I just added a skylight to the pretend room), I was given the choice of either a bed or writing instruments, I'd be sleeping for the rest of my days on a cold floor with a pillow made of crumpled paper. ■

FINAL REVIEW

I. I really tried to make a thoughtful exit.

    a. *Great seeing you guys!*

    b. *I'll for sure text you the name of that shoe website!*

    c. *Oh right, see you at that thing next week!*

    d. Once outside on the sidewalk I realize

        i. I forgot my scarf

        ii. I left it on the table

    e. Now I have to dash back into the gathering

        i. and do that thing where you try to act simultaneously gracious

        ii. and invisible.

II. I purchased a massive box of Q-tips.

    a. Maybe there were a thousand Q-tips in there
        i. Maybe ten million
        ii. I have no idea
    b. Whatever the number, it was a lot, a whole lot, somewhere between excessive and insane
    c. When I put the box away, I thought, *Well, one thing's for sure: I will never, ever have to buy Q-tips again*
    d. I could imagine using one or two a day and then maybe eventually—after twenty years?—getting to the point where I'd make a noticeable dent in the tightly packed layers
    e. But I could not conceive of a time when there would be just a couple left . . . two lone, skinny stragglers flopping around the bottom
    f. But one day, while everyone else was going about their business, I reached in and pulled out the very last Q-tip
    g. The box, as it turns out, was not endless.

III. I am looking at that photo of the three of us.

    a. Just a few hours after delivery

        i. we are so ruddy-skinned

        ii. right out of the gate

        iii. blank slates

    b. Jason is holding the baby

    c. Our expressions seem to say

        i. *Here he is!*

        ii. *Our first baby!*

        iii. *The world's first baby!*

        iv. *All the other babies who exist are rumors, vague versions of a baby!*

        v. *Ours is the only real baby!*

    d. This photo was taken two decades ago

        i. This was when I still had to look up the pediatrician's phone number

        ii. This was when, filling out forms, I'd catch myself writing *Ann*, my own mom's name, in the space for *mother.*

IV. I'd like to be deliberate about what you might associate me with.

    a. Some already associate me with a yellow umbrella

        i. That's fine by me

        ii. I like that

    b. I'm going to toss out another everyday item that also feels good: a doorknob

    c. Doorknob =

        i. small

        ii. give me your hand

        iii. come on in.

V. You just can't compete with the way green treetops look against a blue sky.

To share a photo of green treetops against a blue sky, text **Green blue**.

You will then be prompted to text your photo.

All photos will appear at the website's **Green**/**Blue** gallery.

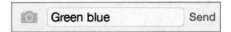

VI. I set up a wish-making portal online.

    a. An image of a dandelion sits next to the wish-making box

    b. When the wisher clicks *submit*, the dandelion blows

    c. The wishes arrive anonymously

    d. Thousands of wishes have been made

    e. Four categories of wishes are tied for most common

        i. money

        ii. happiness

        iii. health

        iv. love

    f. A surprising number of people wish for good weather

        i. Two people wished for rain

    g. A good amount of wishes are about yearning to travel

        i. to Africa

        ii. to Disneyland

        iii. to New York

        iv. to Italy

        v. to the moon

    h. One person wished to be a mermaid

    i. Close your eyes and think about the wishes

        i. Maybe it will help someone's wish come true.

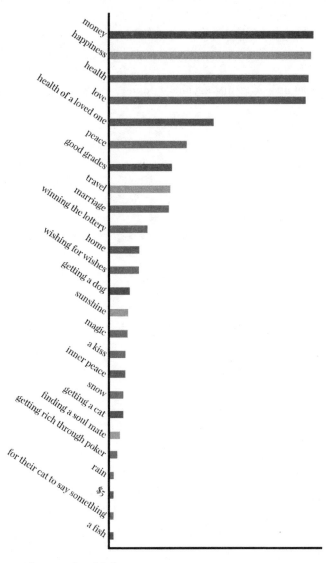

FIG. 1 What people wish for

VII. At the baggage claim I see the man and woman from
my row.

a. *My people! These are my people!*
b. They are now familiar to me
c. We spent three hours elbow-to-elbow
d. We passed plastic cups of ice water and mini bags of
pretzels over to one another
e. I know what they look like asleep
f. Then we hoist our bags off the conveyor belt,
wheel away in scattered directions
i. never to see each other again.

VIII. Sometimes I like to change up my response when Jason
says *I love you.*

    a. *Thank you*, I'll say

    b. Or: *Good to know*

    c. Or: *Phew!*

    d. But usually I say *I love you* back.

IX. I am watching Uncle Henry as he walks away after dinner.

    a. His slow, gentlemanly shuffle along the snowy sidewalk

    b. He looks so dapper

        i. camel hair dress coat

        ii. trilby hat on his head

        iii. wife of sixty years on his arm

    c. Any moment now he will probably call back with his signature send-off

    d. Yes, there it is

        i. *Bye, Ames!*

    e. He was such a good sweet man

    f. His granddaughter is an elementary school teacher and for years he volunteered in her classroom

        i. The children adored him

        ii. They called him Grampy

        iii. When reading stories or sharing tales of his boyhood, he often wept

    g. When he died, those children all came to pay their respects

    h. Everyone who knew him loved him

    i. When my aunt broke the news to their mail carrier she had to bring him inside to sit down

        i. He could not be consoled.

X. I came across Paris's homework on the kitchen counter.

    a. It was a translation practice sheet

    b. Ten simple words

    c. It was her sweet, diligent handwriting that initially caught my eye

       i. I've kept the piece of paper on my desk for years now

    d. Something about these exact words in this exact order

       i. like an accidental mantra

       ii. like a sublime, no-frills distillation of every single book, every single philosophy, every single everything

       iii. like it begs to be recited over and over and over again.

FIG. 1

love	אוֹהֵב .1
hear	שׁוֹמֵעַ .2
See	רוֹאֶה .3
grow	גְּדֵלָה .4
open	פּוֹתֵחַ .5
play	מְשַׂחֶקֶת .6
say	אוֹמֵר .7
eat	אוֹכֵל .8
sing	לָשִׁיר .9
can	יָכוֹל .10

To hear this recited by my daughter all these years later, text **Mantra**.

[📷]	Mantra	Send

XI. In the alley, there is a bright pink flower peeking out
      through the asphalt.

   a. It looks like futility
   b. It looks like hope. ■

END
NOTES

For the musical accompaniment to these last pages,

text **End notes**.

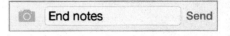

If you were happy before you opened this book, you are probably still happy. If you were medium-fine before, you are probably still generally, existentially a-ok. In both cases, I hope my thoughts have served as a handy amplifier to your own soulful interior humming and strumming. However, if you were sad or troubled before, and that feeling has not eased at all, I am sorry—I wish that this had made everything all right. Tell me what I can do and help me to understand, because I'm guessing here, and I'm ready, and we don't have much time. ■

End Notes

Long ago I was given the advice that it is better to say your good-byes early than to be the last to leave. I was in my late teens at the time, and I remember how counterintuitive those two sensible cents felt to me. *Why would I want to leave when the party's still so fun? I haven't even talked to _____ yet!* Overstaying one's welcome was a more nuanced, grown-up, social-cue concept to grow into, an acquired taste. But I am not sure that age and perspective have nudged me much. If anything, my pendulum is even further out of whack, dangling all the way on the side of leave-kicking-and-screaming. Most holidays and family gatherings conclude the same way: with Jason catching my eye and making a *let's-wrap-it-up* circle in the air with his index finger, followed by him and the kids waiting for me in the car as I try to extricate myself from the night, to come to terms with it being over, to cram in a few more huggy good-byes while the car headlights glare at me through my folks' front window. And by the way, I smile, I do not grimace, thinking about the husband and wife who are always the last to shuffle away from our gatherings. This couple may halfheartedly rev up when they see others departing, but then they just end up lingering with their coats on, wrapped leftovers in hand, sharing just one more great story. ■

Bye. I love you. Thank you. In a last-call, sincere, farewell moment, those are the six words that would fall out of my mouth. I don't think I could even suppress it. In fact, in certain situations, I'd probably repeat it on a loop, like an incantation, as if chanting *byeIloveyouthankyou byeIloveyouthankyou byeIloveyouthankyou* hard and focused enough might actually do the trick of penetrating the constricting haze of language, transmitting (finally!) exact meaning and intent. If, for example, I picture myself as someone immigrating to 1920s America, frantically waving good-bye to my shtetl parents from the deck of an ocean liner as it pushes back from the harbor, I'm shouting (over the ship's loud horn), *Bye, Mama! Bye, Papa! I love you! Thank you! Bye! Thank you! I love you!* If I were a rock star, my post-encore, acronym refrain of choice: *BILYTY! BILYTY!* If I were on my death bed, my family surrounding me, my bony hands holding theirs, I'm shout-whispering, *Bye, guys! I love you so much! Thank you! I love you forever! Bye. I love you. Thank you.* ∎

I was here, you see. I was.[1]

I was so big, bigger every day . . .

And there was a house and a school.

And a car and a job and a dog!

And everything was rush-rush quick,

and hard, so hard.

I wonder. I wonder what was so . . . hard?[2]

We could see our entire world.

And our entire world, at that moment,

was green and golden and perfect.[3]

Guests coming soon.

And still no flowers on table.

I must go into the garden.

I want to go far away.

So many places I never saw.

This is a strange land.

Sun never stops shining.

I am so tired.

I want to sleep but light in my eyes.

Write me.

I want letters waiting.[4]

---

[1] Ending of *Encyclopedia of an Ordinary Life*

[2] Ending of *Elsewhere*, Gabrielle Zevin

[3] Ending of *The Absolutely True Diary of a Part-Time Indian*, Sherman Alexie

[4] Ending of *A Woman of Independent Means*, Elizabeth Forsythe Hailey

I would like it very much if you thought of me
as a mouse telling you a story, this story,
with the whole of my heart
whispering it in your ear in order to
save myself from the darkness,
and to save you from the darkness too.[5]

Good-by. Good-by, world.
Good-by to clocks ticking . . .
And food and coffee.
And new-ironed dresses and hot baths . . .
and sleeping and waking up.
Oh, earth,
you're too wonderful for anybody to realize you.[6]

She came to the door to see me out
and kissed me on both cheeks.[7]
We must keep looking.
I'll be off now.[8]

Bye.
I love you.
Thank you.[9]

---

[5] Ending of *The Tale of Despereaux*, Kate DiCamillo
[6] Ending of *Our Town*, Thornton Wilder
[7] Ending of *The Razor's Edge*, W. Somerset Maugham
[8] Ending of *The Diving Bell and the Butterfly*, Jean-Dominique Bauby
[9] Ending of *Textbook Amy Krouse Rosenthal* ■